Moonlight Confessions

Heartfelt collection of poems dedicated to themes of love & loss

Written by Karin Cho

Artwork by Winny Chen

Absolute Author
Publishing House

Moonlight Confessions

Copyright © 2020

Karin Cho

Publisher: Absolute Author Publishing House

Library of Congress Cataloging-in-Publication Data

Cho, Karin

Moonlight Confessions / Karin Cho

ISBN: 978-1-64953-061-5

Dedicated to my younger self, I promised I'd someday make you proud.

Here are a few of my favorite pieces of writing dedicated to the themes of love and loss.

Introduction

I have spent the majority of my life questioning whether or not I was cursed with misfortune and bad luck. It all began with a rocky childhood with a neglectful mother who constantly reminded me how useless I was as a person. If that was not already challenging enough, my parents did not speak English fluently and like many second-generation Americans, I never learned my parents' native language. Oftentimes, the way to communicate was with broken English/Korean and Google Translate. Subsequently, this developed a barrier between us due to the lack of connection and understanding. It was a discomforting feeling to know that I was unable to feel heard even with people who share my own blood. Growing up, I lacked emotional stability and confidence from my deep-rooted feelings of inadequacy. In addition to the constant reminder that I could never do anything right, I was very well aware that I could not even speak to my own parents the way other children could.

As a child, I developed an anxious attachment style that originated with my attachment to my mother and in turn, was constantly needy for her attention and care. I can see very clearly how her irresponsible behavior caused problems in my development as I was unable to be alone, to hang out with my friends without feeling home sick, and unable to attend summer camps or sleepovers the way my peers would. My mother would frequently drop me off at her friend's houses while she gambled in casinos hours away from me. As many children may know, days without a parent can feel like an eternity and my fear of abandonment ignited from this uncertainty of whether or not my mother would come back. I felt deeply wounded as I consistently endorsed the belief that I had been betrayed, abandoned, and lied to. Furthermore, I did not have a phone back then to ask when she would come back, which only compounded the belief that I had been left behind.

The worst times were when she dropped me off at church retreats where I would be surrounded by strangers without any knowledge of what was going on. I was told I would only be staying for a couple of hours when in actuality, I was taken to a different state on a bus filled with strangers I had never met. I would then be forced to stay and participate in church activities for days. I associate these events with some of the most uneasy and uncomfortable feelings I had ever faced. To demonstrate the intensity of these aversive feelings, I would fake injuries in the hopes that the counselors could call my mother for me. She would pick up the phone and assure me that she would be right there, but she never came until the retreat was over. I gradually learned not to trust words, a lesson that stuck with me throughout young adulthood.

The anxiety of being left behind escalated to the point where I used to tie my wrist with her wrist with rope while she was sleeping so that when she would get out of bed in the morning, I would be able to feel the pull of the rope and stop her before she left again. Before the school bus would arrive to pick me up for school, I would frantically ask my mother if she would be home to let me in the house when I came back because there were countless times when she would not be there to open the door for me.

Consequently, I would wait in my backyard, feeling abandoned yet again. My panic would arise so frequently that I had even created a secret code word with my family friends who understood my convoluted fears. This code word would indicate to them to notify an adult nearby that I was having a panic attack. Childhood was not an easy era and unfortunately, my teenage years were not any better. In addition to not being attractive, I failed the majority of my high school classes and worst of all, my relationships suffered from having no boundaries with people.

I was deeply deprived of nurture and an understanding of my own emotional needs. As a result, I sabotaged every single one of my relationships. In a nutshell, my high school journey was not a pleasant one. I was largely unaware of the fact that I was being, "Too much" when I would shamelessly express my love to those I was attracted to. I was desperate to feel this so-called feeling of true love, so when I thought I found it, I would chase it-chase it until it made me look like a fool. I was unaware of the consequences of being scrutinized and harshly judged by those I wanted approval from. My insecurities only intensified from the ongoing rumors about me and my need for attention from boys. These rumors completely disregarded who I was as a person and were insensitive to my personal battles.

I always felt like the ugly one in my family, the stupid girl in math class, and the obsessive fangirl who was desperate for every guy's attention. A salient memory I have is one that involved me finding out that some boys took my math binder filled with my failed exams and posted it in the boy's locker room for everyone else to see and mock. This was the type of embarrassment I faced on a daily basis. I already felt insecure enough and this certainly did not help with my low self-esteem. I continued living life believing that I had no value and that the world was a cruel and uncaring void that got a kick out of seeing me fail.

As I got older, the anxious attachment I developed permeated into my romantic relationships. I was eager to jump into the dating world, oblivious to the dangers of men's predatory behaviors and determined to finally have my emotional needs met.

And then I met him.

I was a junior in high school when I met him and I thought to myself, "Is this the universe's attempt to finally give me the love that I deserve? Is my luck finally turning around?"

I was dead wrong.

He just so happened to be my very first experience with physical, sexual, and emotional abuse. I experienced two years of agony and deep emotional pain from cheating, lying, assault, and rape. There were so many nights where I would feel like drowning in my own puddles of tears from my crying spells, frozen in my bed as I ached and ached for life to get better. I sought professional help in school and met with a social worker every day for five consecutive months. There had been moments when my situation had gotten so intense that I would be allowed to skip all my classes for the day to focus on receiving help right away. It felt like a sick joke: the one time a boy was interested in me, he turned out to be an abusive cheater who robbed me of my innocence.

Upon my college admission, I was hopeful that I could get a fresh start in life. Although I was still depressed, I had enough resilience to push myself to look forward to a new life away from my unstable home environment and traumatic memories. Unfortunately, I faced another terrible year of hardships, gossip, and negativity from my peers yet again. I had been physically assaulted by strangers on the streets near my college campus, and as I was laying there looking over next to me to see my friend bleeding, I once again asked myself the same question I had asked years ago, "Why me?" It seemed like no matter how kind I was, how gentle I was, or how genuine I tried to be with others, I came to the conclusion that the universe simply wanted to see me suffer. Throughout college, I had put in a greater amount of effort to work on my physical appearance and therefore no longer felt like "The ugly girl." Although I felt more confident with my appearance, I still felt that deep sense of inadequacy except this time, it was hidden behind make-up and filters.

I was reintroduced to drugs during my early college years and recklessly chased after the feelings that drugs would elicit. I was desperate to feel any sense of happiness, even at the cost of destroying my brain and body. During my sophomore year of college, if I was not taking Xanax to help with my anxiety, I was swallowing MDMA pills to feel some sense of euphoria to experience just a few hours of pure ecstasy and bliss. One night, I had recklessly taken too many drugs and ended up in the emergency room, where I was in desperate need of medical attention. As harrowing and excruciating the overdose had felt on my body and mind, I also felt a sense of comfort in knowing that this may be the end of all the trauma and hurt I had previously experienced. I was ready to go because it occurred to me that if I was going to die someday, it might as well be now.

I survived.

I survived even if a part of me did not want to. I was previously contemplating suicide every day for a while and skipping classes because I was no longer able to walk those hallways and encounter the people who had hurt me. I was on the edge, dangling my feet to the bottomless pit of my own death. At that point, I felt that I tried everything. I even dialed multiple suicide hotlines only for the person on the other line to hang up on me in the middle while I was crying for help. As a result, I wrote goodbye letters to the few people in my life who cared for me. But even throughout the darkest of times, there was a tiny nagging voice in my head nudging me not to die *just yet*. I had felt so low that a part of me felt that the only possible direction left was upwards.

Contrary to that belief, my life was not an uphill battle. Rather, it was a downward spiral of chaos and instability. Yet, I did not give up. Despite all the emotional damage I endured, I fantasized about a future where I was admired, loved, and respected. All I longed for was a shot at life where *I* was the superhero of my own story. There was a raging fire in me that wanted justice from all the pain I had to suffer from other people's irresponsible behaviors. I did not know what to do with the burden of intense emotion and pain that had accumulated throughout my childhood and adolescence. I had no health insurance and the therapy that was offered within the university counseling center was simply not enough. The counselors gave me their opinion and suggested I seek extra help off-campus with someone who had more time to dedicate to me. Additionally, I was suggested to take medication multiple times but declined each time.

Every decision I ever made was with the intention with never being left behind from the ones I loved most. In desperate cases, I would send massive amounts of money to whoever I wanted comfort from, as a desperate cry for help. These are only the few things my instability and deep fear of abandonment had caused in my life. Shameful moments like these were moments I could never take back and have had to learn with the fact that I was going to be judged, misunderstood, and looked down upon from the ones I cherished most.

In every single aspect of my life- whether it be family, social, school, or relationships, I felt an empty void. I found it peculiar that I would always cry when I saw my baby photos because I would be reminded of the times when I was a sweet and innocent child who was unaware of the horrors of life. I would have done anything to obtain that sense of innocence again. I felt terrible for the innocent child in me whose body should never have been violated and forced upon. It breaks my heart to rewind to the helplessness that I had felt that night, the night where I could do nothing but remain frozen as my body was being salvaged for his own pleasure.

I remember that night. I witnessed my innocence leave my body after it happened. If I could have it my way, I would not have wanted it to leave that soon, or at least not like that. Afterwards, I just laid there, sobbing in extreme pain while my rapist slept comfortably next to me, like a baby. Coping with trauma is not simple. During these devastating times, I felt so small. Voice-less, really.

So, I started to write.

I began to journal my emotions and my therapist recommended that I gradually get into the habit of diving deep into my psyche and past. I began to feel comfortable in describing my emotions, a feeling that was new to me. I *needed* to express this fire that I felt and did so by writing it all down. Upon confiding in my sister, I decided to change my major to journalism to focus on writing. Subsequently, I enrolled in classes where I was no longer "The stupid girl," but rather, the star student. I eventually became the version of myself that I wished I was back when I was a child. With the help of mental health professionals, my older sister, professors who saw my potential, and amazing friends who inspired me, I can proudly say that I blossomed into the woman I am today.

I dedicated myself to transforming my pain into pieces of writing. I began to believe that through every god-awful event I experienced, there was solace in healing. From those traumatic experiences, I was able to create articles that touched people's hearts and empowered those who faced similar hardships in life. Sexual assault, beatings, cheating, and emotional abuse- all these unfortunate events that I never asked for, as much as I dread replaying those memories, there is something beautiful in experiencing life so intensely. I, without a doubt, have an interesting journey and have a tremendous story to share. I am now completely sober, and now understand that my experiences have created a person with an endless amount of insight to life. Consequently, I have the unique ability to articulate meaningful interpretations of life and emotions. As expected, I still have challenging days, but I feel comfort in knowing that I no longer feel like a hostage to my own mind.

The child in me who felt abandoned and hurt is still me. The teenage girl who was beaten, raped, and on the edge of death is *still me*, and I embody all the different parts of myself. I owe it to the child in me to become the best person I could possibly be, for the Karin who was suffering all alone in the dark. I am here to say that I am here for you and *I will never abandon you*.

Ironically, I feel a sense of wholeness and this stems from the empty feelings I previously faced. I am now admired by my peers for my intellect, my ability to articulate my feelings, my vulnerability, and my willingness to embrace who I am as an individual. I can proudly state that I only earn straight A's and also established my identity on Medium by honing my craft as a writer. I even came to terms with my mother's unconventional parenting style and have forgiven her for her mistakes. I slowly grew to love her as an individual and better understand her own psyche. All the hardships I faced created a strong, passionate, and resilient individual who was somehow able to transmute her suffering into strength and I encourage everyone to embark on the beautiful and terrifying journey of self-improvement.

"Can You Meet Me At The Top?"

I'm at the top of the mountain now, I've been chasing mountains ever since I met you. The day I met you... If only I knew it was the last time I'd see you again.

You're not by my side anymore. I wish you were here; sharing this incredible moment with me. It felt like a scene right out of a movie

Something majestic was in the air that night, I felt it.

Thank you for being the first and only man who ever asked me if I could be their girlfriend with enough warmth, it could last me an entire winter.

As I rewind, my heart pours out for you more and more.

Even the way we met; serendipity.

April 19th 2015, the night I had the privilege of meeting you online.

No mutuals, nowhere near me, yet we found each other.

Thankful.

What were the chances? I think God spent extra time planning that part of my life because it felt so right,

Like the last missing puzzle piece to a complete finish.

Your sign: Gemini, My sign: Sagittarius.

They say they are like a match made in heaven, soulmate connection.

My time with you was snatched away from me like a stuffed teddy bear being ripped apart from a child's arms

Without warning,

It hurt.

You were mine, I had no doubts

No insecurity, no anxiety, no panic

Just euphoria in all of my senses. Cloud nine and above.

I wish I could trust a person like that again but I won't,

I haven't.

I still remember our ritual every day, 9–10pm we met on Skype

I'd play Stolen Dance on repeat and we'd talk about anything and everything.

"The only thing I feel is pain caused by absence of you."

"We have to fetch back the time, they have stolen from us."

I came to the realization years later, the song that was stuck in my head at the time just happened to describe the exact feelings I had felt for you then.

There was a reason I always looped that specific song all along I suppose, maybe it was my unconscious mind trying to connect with yours.

Before you, I had been judged and treated terribly by the boys around me.

None of that mattered after I met you.

Skype was filled with hours and hours of playful conversations, eye smiles, and dreams of someday meeting.

Oftentimes, I wouldn't even show my face during the calls, but that didn't stop you from connecting with me.

Most teenage guys only want to see a visual, but you were different.

There was a special moment that I will never forget. The day you nonchalantly joked about meeting me on your birthday,

I cried.

I think that was the first time I felt both extreme sadness and happiness at the same time.

Sadness: How would it happen? You didn't have your license, you were in another state, and I had never been on a date before. Please don't get my hopes up high.

Happiness: You wanted to see me. Initiative. Could it really happen?

It happened.

Day of, I wore my favorite outfit and rehearsed lines with a friend so I could perfect every angle of my face before I'd meet you.

Insecure.

I was deeply insecure but that day, I was ready to be confident.

June 5th: Today's the day. It's also your birthday,

Thank god for your existence.

Pacing back and forth, I send you a photo of myself,

No filter, no edits, just natural Karin.

I glance outside and see a blue license plate,

It's you.

I walk to the front of my house entrance and hide in the corner

Slowly, your car arrives and I instantly feel like throwing up.

My very first date.

Sneaking out to a different state with a boy I met online,

It was the most teenager thing I had ever done.

I open the car door and for the first time,

You are no longer on a computer screen, miles away

You're an inch apart from me and reality begins to dissolve

Every moment feels more and more surreal, as if I'm on a acid trip straight to heaven

I remember your outfit, your long lanky body and that adorable beauty mark next to your eye,

I have the same one too.

Your eyes: Achingly beautiful puppy eyes, my absolute favorite feature of yours.

Your aura, Genuine. Gentle. Graceful.

You drive, you brake too hard, I yank forward and you apologize immediately.

GPS in between us, below the car window.

Your phone case: Red.

Yes, I remember all the details.

I notice in the backseat, you brought your hoodie for me

I wear it till this day, thank you.

3 hours to another state: Simsbury, Connecticut.

We pick up your best friend and his girlfriend. The first thing he mentions is that I resemble your mother.

I cared for her even though I didn't know her

I always wanted to meet her,

I never got to.

I step out of the car, I'm tiny.

You tower over me and our jokes on Skype about our height difference finally make a reappearance.

This time, it's funnier.

We walk in the movie theater, you pay for me.

I lightly push you, you didn't have to!

You already drove six hours and paid for tolls, you were so kind to that toll-man.

You pay for a drink, popcorn, and our tickets.

Gentleman.

We sit in the theater. I've never been this close to a guy before.

You put your arm around me, and for the first time in my life,

I feel lightning in my veins, electricity in my palms, and fire in my lungs.

I can feel all of life's elements within my own body,

All from your touch.

I question if this is what love feels like.

You ask if I'm comfortable with the arm rest poking me

I lie.

I don't care how uncomfortable the seats are,

My heart is alive,

My soul is touched,

And my life is at its peak.

Movie ends.

We walk out of the theater and our clumsy bodies gravitate toward each other like magnets in love.

My emotions explode like fireworks as I examine your dreamy face once again,

You're beautiful.

By the way, I don't know if anyone has ever told you,

Your eyes resemble rainbows when you smile and when you let yourself go and smile with teeth,

I feel my heart beats a little bit faster, with purpose.

Our jokes are finally coming to life, everything is in harmony.

You get up because of a phone call from mom, I find it sweet that you take her calls even when you're with friends,

She matters to you.

I admire you even when you're on the phone, unaware of how flawless you are.

We leave.

Your friends also leave the car, it's finally just us two again.

VANIC x K. FLAY — CAN'T SLEEP plays in the background

"I love you so much, I'm staying here all night

Don't want to get up, I don't want to stop, I don't want to close my eyes."

I waited a lifetime for this moment, to see you in person. So I snap away, capturing every enticing angle of you.

There is no weirdness or judgement of my overly affectionate attitude,

Thank you for that.

For months, you'd tell me stories about visiting mountains and embracing the view,

It's finally my turn to visit the mountain with you.

You park your car and I immediately notice how dark it is.

You give me your hoodie, grab my hand and lead me up the mountain.

I see marks on the trees and you teach me that's how you find your way when hiking up to the top.

Thank you, a lesson I always remembered.

We crash into each other every few seconds, unable to let go of each other's bodies.

Woah. Did you hear that? We look up. It's a deer.

It's right in front of us, staring blankly at our faces. We're both frozen in our tracks, I've never seen a deer in person before.

Note to self: This is truly a magical night.

I make eye contact with you and the word that comes to mind is

Home.

I think about how I'm hours away from my house, in a town I've never been in and yet, I feel like I'm home.

Something about seeing the deer on our way to the top aligns with my belief that this is exactly where I am supposed to be.

We make it to the top.

Breathtaking, the view is...

It leaves us

Speechless.

Our bodies collide with each other as we gaze at the mountain top in awe and appreciation.

It hits me,

The feeling of finally being next to the person you have only seen on a screen for months is simply indescribable.

Dopamine dancing in my brain.

I think back to the day we first met online by chance,

Mental note: The best things in life happen when we least expect it.

I cannot emphasize how perfect this scene is right now, if there's a maximum level of happiness; This is it.

I am living it at this very moment with you.

We lay on the mountain floor and stare at the stars as Snow (Hey Oh) — Red Hot Chili Peppers plays in the background.

I position myself up, stare into your puppy eyes and cover half your face with your beanie in a silly manner.

I go for it, I kiss you.

You're caught off guard but you enjoy it, we lock lips and you are officially my first kiss,

No regrets.

We then exchange I love you's for the first time in person,

I love you.

My emotions are dreaming and I don't want to wake up.

You call out my full name and my innocent eyes twinkle as you politely ask, "Will you, Karin Cho, be my girlfriend?"

I couldn't have asked for a more romantic scene with the one I love.

The agony of separation and long distance has finally come to an end,

We graciously leave the mountain after I ecstatically agree to being your girlfriend.

Before we go far, you stop and zip up my hoodie and protect me from the dark.

It's now 5 years later.

I never saw you again.

I never felt that way again.

I never trusted that hard again.

I'm at the mountain top

Waiting.

I made it all on my own this time, following the marked trees just like you taught me.

I'm at the top of the mountain now, I've been chasing mountains ever since I met you.

The day I met you... If only I knew it was the last time I'd see you again.

You're not by my side anymore, I wish you were here; sharing this incredible moment with me.

"Açai Bowls"

I stroll into the new bakery on my block that I hear has a pink interior design, an absolute *must* for me. I order an açai bowl and situate myself in the corner. I generally lean toward sitting in corners, close to the walls and liberated from interaction. I'm munching on the savory granola and coconut strips as I notice a familiar face walk in.

Suddenly, I'm not in a cozy cafe anymore. My heart rewinds back to the last time I saw you, a time period so ancient I nearly overlooked the sentiment of wistfulness. In this moment, it doesn't make a difference how long it has been since we last connected because your essence has consistently felt timeless. The air almost feels translucent and dreamlike, as I try to grasp at the conscious realization that *you* are really, *really*, here. To be honest, I'd always felt your spirit, even after we separated, but even more so now. And as I observe *you* from my corner across the room, I can feel the burning chemistry illuminate, as our childhood selves *reconnect* as one.

...Can it be? Is it really *you?*

My gaze is frozen stuck at the entryway, still in blissful shock that from head to toe, *you* are here. My fingers tap nervously against the wooden table in an uneven staccato, as I question all of life's *serendipity* trying with every effort to make the connection, that even after everything and all that's happened, everything *must* happen for a reason.

I get up from my seat, braced against my own two feet, and feel the still hesitation between running to *you* and running *away.*

...This was all I ever wanted.

For years upon years, this moment, *this* reunion...this was all I had ever ached for. The amount of tears I shed, over the course of a lifetime, *waiting,* for this...it could fill an ocean.

I pause. I try to swallow the lump in my throat and sit back down. Returning to my seat, I reminisce about the nights we can't relive and dreams that we just couldn't make happen. You observe your surroundings and lock eyes with me in a delicate moment that feels like an eternity.

Like clockwork, everyone else in the room begins to dissolve away, one by one, *as if they were smoke to begin with* until the only two people present in this universe are *you & me.*

Your eyes, the puppy-like glow of innocence but trained *always,* with a sharp demeanor.

You break your gaze and look away. I try to remember how to breathe but I don't want to let go of the air of this very moment. Not again.

It's been years now, and I wouldn't be surprised if the woman sitting before you feels like a *stranger* to the girl that you had *once* fallen in love with.

I try to shake the disbelief from my eyes and pray that you don't fall away like the rest of the smoke. At this point, I'm thinking that I may have seen a ghost. Are you even real? Or do you only exist as a delusion borne out of all the years I had spent longing to see you again.

I pinch myself to make sure I wasn't dreaming.

You're real, it's you.

You stroll towards me, and the room no longer scents like fruits and coffee anymore, it smells like fresh laundry infused with bits of lavender; your natural scent. I nearly collapse in my seat as I feel the pressure created by every step as you slowly make your way toward me.

The sunlight from outside casts a radiant glow through the glass windows and shines toward your direction.

And before I have any time to rehearse any kind of speech in my head of what to say to someone like you in a moment like this

Suddenly, you're before me, toe to toe, smiling down at the girl who had been waiting, patiently, for you, *all along.*

I work my eyes up slowly, across every wrinkle of your shirt, every line of your body, until my own gaze meets yours. This is the first occasion when we'd be in the same room together since we were kids. Your mere presence has my hands shaking, uncontrollably, and knees weak and wobbling, as I battle to maintain eye contact with you

"Karin?" you softly ask…

Your angelic face lights up with joy as I feel the knots in my stomach grip and tighten, turning and turning as each second passes.

"Oh my god! What are you doing here?"

I exclaim as my entire body shoots up from my seat and darts to your warm embrace. A hug that felt *more* than just a hug, so much more. The closeness reminds me of all the intimacy we once entangled ourselves in, back when our teenage selves were intoxicated in young love. I desperately hang onto you as I remember all the times I'd wear your sweatshirt, in hopes that it would replace the feeling of being with you.

"What are the odds?"

You ask, ending the sincere hug and sitting me down, back in my corner and wooden table. And as I push my seat toward yours, I *surrender* all of my years of patience and simply confess,

"I thought about you every day, how are you?"

You slowly look down at the table as the words leave my mouth, and then you recast your focused expression to the doorway,

She appears. She looks like me.

She notices you and immediately, you stand up, smile and greet her with a romantic hug I knew a thousand times before her.

You awkwardly introduce us and in that very moment, my expectations and hopes *sink* all at once, drowning in thrashing, violent waters to a shallow grave. You'd think in this moment, I'd feel an immense amount of jealousy and anger, yet I don't.

Instead, I feel my childhood hopes and dreams shattered into a million pieces.

I feel nothing but pure sadness.

I watch you two gently hold hands in front of me.

Holding hands... Your hands were the *first* hands I had ever held, romantically, back when we were kids. The flashbacks continue to play, but with a melancholic undertone this time around.

You both smile, lightly, and as she makes her way to the cashier to place her order, I quickly pack my belongings and throw out my açai bowl. The same açai bowl I always loved... It no longer tastes sweet like the way I remembered it; it now tastes bitter.

What changed? I ask myself, confused with how my favorite dessert can so quickly rot in a matter of seconds.

Before I leave, I look back at you one *final* time. We share one *last* silent moment of nothing but pure *eye contact.*

We take a final breathe in this cherished moment, as we both *silently* communicate to one another in *spirit,*

"...*Until we meet again, old friend.*"

"Dream Sequence"

I dreamt of us last night

We sat side by side together at a family restaurant

My hand, instinctually reaching for yours

Underneath the table, in front, and even on your lap

I never have to wait long for your arrival, as you're always a doorstep away

Even when you're speaking to the waiter

Focused on another human being,

Your hand doesn't leave mine

My heart feels filled, so filled it overflows

Like a sad lake crying in its home

How sweet it feels, from a gesture

so lighthearted, so subtle

You see, it's more than simply holding hands

It's the understanding of my needs

The synchronicity of togetherness

The acceptance of my overwhelming affection

Bittersweet to know, in that alternate universe

I was loved

"False Reality"

I'm in love with someone who doesn't exist

You're simply a memory, one I can barely make out

Even if I wanted to,

I wouldn't be able to map out who you are anymore.

It's been too long,

I'm in love with a ghost

The individual in my dream is you,

The you I created in my mind,

Meticulously designed to fit my idea of perfection.

But in reality, it's not actually you.

Maybe that's what dreams are for

A giant mirror reflecting back our hopes and desires

When I wake up, I am crushed with the true reality that exists today

You are sand, slipping through the cracks of my palm

As I desperately try to keep you intact in this dimension.

Year by year, a piece of you dies from my memory

All I have left are past photos as proof that you actually existed

Side by side with me, there was once a time where we were one.

But every time I'm sure of it,

Every time I'm certain you're real

I wake up and open my eyes

And lay in bed questioning if you ever existed at all

"Liquid Gold"

My friends tell me my lovers all look alike,

Little do they know, those men started with you

I once thought I had a type

Truthfully, I believe I'm attempting to recreate

The love we once lost

I've gone mad.

I can't stop the ruminations,

The constant fixations,

A broken record on repeat.

A broken record on repeat.

A broken record on repeat.

I am liquid gold, pouring for everyone to see

But I'm waiting to be claimed by you

Divine destruction, anticipation for your attention

To notice, to keep me

As I've kept you,

Maybe just maybe

If I turned to liquid gold

It would have been enough this time around

Enough,

For you to have stayed

"Class"

Rewind to High School, I was that girl

The only Asian failing math class

Labeled stupid, dumb, failure,

I took these labels home with me every day

Walking around this earth with a deep sense of lack

All the other girls, boasting about their AP courses and straight A's

Boys drooling to get a taste, while I refused to raise my hand

Even though my mind was racing with answers

My voice, desperate to crawl out of its burning throat

My failed grades once found in the boy's locker room,

Posted, for everyone to see

Humiliation.

They say the eyes are the windows to the soul, though my eyes were long shattered from inadequacy and hurt

Past lover of mine once compared me to another girl, emphasizing her intelligence right to my face, describing her as the ideal woman

It made me feel so small, like I hardly existed

Fast forward years later

Journalism class, my junior year

First day of introductions and I see you

You're sitting in front of me with a spiffy suit on and I am immediately intimidated by your magnetic confidence and glowing radiance

You introduce yourself and reveal your hopes in becoming a lawyer,

A profession I have always felt too stupid to pursue

A profession I dreamed of

I look up to you.

Weeks pass and you participate every time

Your voice, always in demand of the room

I always listen in when you speak, I can listen to you speak all day.

It's almost effortless for you,

I think to myself how I hope someday

To be just like you

Charismatic, polite, and able to hold eye contact for longer than three seconds,

How do you do it?

I notice in class that you always nod when others are speaking, I appreciate that.

Another week passes of unsaid feelings and each glance at your face is a weekly reminder of how badly I want to speak to you.

Today's class is on debating the innocence and morality of a journalist we read about earlier in the week

Everyone gets in a circle, I purposely sit right next to you.

The professor tells us to pick a side and support it with evidence, the lawyer in me is pumped to see how this will all go down

Deeply attracted to intelligence and wit, I already know your comments will be my favorite

To my surprise, I quickly realize I am the underdog with the unpopular stance.

Nobody else agrees with what I have to say,

But I fight anyway

The first time I ever let my guard down in a classroom

I speak my mind and like word vomit,

My opinions pour out of my mouth

Everyone shakes their head in disagreement and I can feel the tension in the room arise as I
slowly regret my decision to speak up

But you, you nod, you hear me out.

You chime in every few seconds to add your thoughts, every comment of yours is perfectly said.

Our very first interaction.

My hands begin to shake underneath the desk as you turn to my side and say,

"I'm really sorry if I keep interrupting, I actually really like what you have to say."

You look deep into my insecure eyes and remain eye contact without hesitation.

Something I could never do.

Years and years of insecurity, pain, and hurt

Gone

Just like that, I received the utmost validation I had ever needed.

I felt empowered, listened to, and respected.

And of all people, for it to be you

You don't even know, how much that day meant to me

All my life, I was unable to reach the top shelf

But for once, I didn't feel small that day.

Every time I pass this classroom, I reminisce about that unforgettable day.

In the midst of a heated debate,

When I was all alone in my beliefs,

You saw something special in me,

Thank you for that.

I speak my mind now,

Every time

"Killer"

What is it about innocence that warms my heart to its core until my eyes start to shed haunted tears

Perhaps it began with my first, the one who stole my innocence, betrayed my trust and salvaged my body as if it was his to ruin

No means no,

But to him it was a trophy, like how serial killers possess trophies after each thrilling kill to remind them of their victims and murderous power

Overpowering me was his trophy. His ego, his pride of believing he was a man

Every letter his villain mouth pronounced was a lie,

Yet

I'm grateful. I'm grateful for the hurt he caused.

For damaged people tend to have a crack in their beaming hearts that allow for more light to reach them and others.

I'm free now

Sprinting toward the finish line, recovering from the hell I once lived through

My killer is still out there, he's far from the finish line

He hadn't even bought the right shoes to begin running

I guess he was too busy belittling me to know

I'm the fastest on the team

I'll proudly beat him at every race, while he sits on the bleachers

Watching me out-run him

Or perhaps he doesn't even notice

As he's too focused on

Plotting his next kill

"Human"

When I woke up to your goodbye text, my heart wailed so intensely, no other organ could function

My eyes, a cascade streaming down my face, wetting my trembling hands as I brushed every tear away to clearly read what had been sent

A hundred times over, in hopes that if I did this long enough, I'd wake up and none of it would be real

But when there was no catch, when the words sent to me were true, I laid in bed, paralyzed from head to toe

Not again, I whimpered.

A broken child waiting for her mother, now a broken woman waiting for her love to return

The memories began to hijack my mind as if I was being forced to watch the same movie

Over and over again,

I couldn't get a break. All my senses, victim to your hold

Sight, scent, taste, touch, and sound.

When you left, it wasn't just you who left

It was all the haunting memories of previous abandonment that coalesced in a bonfire of unhealed wounds

So when I say it hurt when you left, what I meant to say is that I forgot how to live

I had to reteach myself

How to breathe

How to eat a meal,

How to sleep at night,

How to cry it out,

How to let go,

How to be human

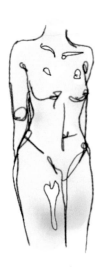

"Kisses"

My kiss is a love letter
Stamped by my affection
Sent to your heart's location
No return address
Open the invitation
Read in between the lines
Feel every vowel
My lips express
Against yours
Word by word
Signed,
Yours truly

"Ecstasy"

You are ecstasy,
My personal
Happy little pill
Capable of extreme euphoria
And supreme destruction

"Meet me halfway"

If I come to breakfast
Will you stay for dinner
If I spend the night
Will you make the bed
If I say I love you
Will you say it back

"Love Withdrawals"

My therapist compared me to an addict,
Unable to let go and function
Until I get my fix
I feel symmetrical when I'm with you,
Perfectly aligned and balanced
A seesaw in still motion,
But the second you're gone
The cravings begin
I no longer feel like a mirror image
Of who I am, Of who I should be
Asymmetrical
Like abstract art,
Something's missing
Shattered pieces, lacking symmetry
Dying to be put back in place
To feel normal,
Alive,
Anything but broken

"Take Off"

My emotions are both
Beauty and beast
Fire and ice
I've been told that
I'm too much
All my life
Too sensitive,
Too deep,
Too emotional,
I believe it's my greatest weapon
The winning kill at every battle
When I first met you
I felt my emotions rising once again
Like an airplane getting ready for takeoff
Though this was a ride
I knew was going to crash
And before I could fasten my seatbelt
I turn to you and ask,
Do you think I'm too much?
Expecting the usual response
No,
I think you're passionate
You reply.
That was the first time,
I made the landing
Flawlessly with no turbulence
Or delay in sight,
To my desired destination
A location
I had always longed for

"Times I fell for you"

When you compared yourself to a fish
Swimming the opposite direction from all the other fishes,
I understand the feeling.
When you held the door for me after our first conversation
I'm sorry I didn't say anything to you then,
You had me speechless.
When you remembered my birthday,
You only ever remember the special ones.
When you picked up on my sharp memory,
Nobody else ever does.
When I saw paintings and album covers plastered all over your wall,
I saw a piece of you displayed in each and every one of them.
When you read my tarot cards,
Nobody ever offers to read mine.
When you told me the name of your car,
Magnolia.
When you met up with me when I needed you
That day,
Our eyes met each other for the first time.
When you noticed the details on my face
The beauty mark above my lip,
To be exact
The subtle designs God created
Tend to go unnoticed,
But you noticed.
When you told me you used to have a stutter
And overcame it by practicing every day,
You're the best speaker I know.
When we hugged for the last time,
I typically jerk away from hugs
I stayed a second too long for yours.
When you told me you want a girl who can steal a painting,
I never wanted to commit a crime so badly.
In fact,
I'm on my way to the MoMA right now
Join me, you can be the lookout

"Secrets"

I've always been a night owl,
Intrigued by the unknown
When midnight strikes
Vulnerabilities appear
Mask of normality slips,
I look out my window
Make love to the moon
Whisper sweet nothings in its ear
Caress its fluorescent face,
Until he shines bright
For the whole world to see
The moon knows all my secrets,
But you know more

"Happy Valentines"

It's the most loving time of the year
Chocolates carefully wrapped around in heart shaped boxes,
Rose petals dripping in romance
Teddy bears, the height of skyscrapers
Hand written cards all ending in
I love you.
When I got ready for my first valentines with you
The last thing I was expecting was tragedy
Yet that's how the night ended.
I was still in high school when it happened,
When I suffocated in the corner of the room
Smothered in your unwanted embrace
Twenty minutes for you,
An eternity of trauma for me
When I look back at that fateful day,
All I wanted was to celebrate
The trauma flashes here and there
But I've learned to turn off the light
The only memory left is the teddy bear I have in my room
I keep it till this day
Despite the cruel memories associated with it
And I know you're wondering
Why I would keep a gift from the devil himself
The stuffed bear is the only reminder left
Of the child, Of the innocence
That I once possessed.
I watch the bear slowly but surely fall apart as the years go by
Decaying in my room as the once beloved gift becomes
An ancient artifact of my ability to trust,
To love again
I wept so hard that night
I could taste the terror in my tears
Feel the betrayal from the blood underneath
A secret so poisonous, its venom burns the tip of my tongue each time I attempt
To reveal what happened to me on valentines day

"Abuse"

The first time he hit me, it was a supposed accident
A misunderstanding, as he called it.
A punch straight to the gut, a forbidden memory
Imprisoned in the basement of my mind,
No visitors are allowed.
The next time he hit me,
He threw a bottle at my face,
Wetting my entire body
Drenched and degraded.
I asked for an extra T-shirt,
He refused to give me one.
I remember when he locked me in his bathroom to exert his power,
I had no say in when I got to leave.
Perhaps that's why I got into the habit of
Staying.
Common sense became backwards
Emotions were my only sense of direction,
It's no wonder I felt so lost back then.
What good is a broken compass anyway
It's unbelievable what can happen behind closed doors
Doors that were locked so securely in the dark
Nobody had a clue,
What could possibly be on the other side.
I've been told that I have grey clouds above me,
Wherever I go
But what do you expect when you've been infected for so long
An infection that has no cure
I decorate myself with a lot of pink,
In hopes it could brighten my dark character.
My favorite color since childhood
The only color that heals me
I don't know how to be
Pain is what I wore every day, for years upon years
I'm trying on different outfits now
I really am,
Nothing quite fits

"Notebook 2.0"

When you held my body up toward the pouring rain
I knew we were stronger than The Notebook
No script
No cameras
Pure bliss, in real time
The rain droplets kissing my body
In sync with your lips against mine
Tears of happiness streaming down my cheek,
Mimicking the love drops from above
You could taste my devotion
I've been through enough storms in life
This one, none like the rest
You are my rainbow
My iridescent light in the darkest hour
The reason it's always worth it
Despite the gravity of thrashing rain
Let's experience more storms together
Hand in hand
Not in fear of the ferocious storms
Or the chaos of downpour
But instead,
In the presence of danger
In the name of love
Risking it all, as always
Head first, hearts in
For this moment,
For us

"Half"

You no longer look at me the same
I've become an old photograph you've seen
A million times before
Nothing special
I call your name over
But your name no longer sounds like a promise I want to keep
Instead, a lie I feel obligated to tell
You let out a sigh
Then reluctantly come by my side
A presence I haven't felt in forever
I could feel our chemistry withering away
you and i
We both know it's time to say goodbye
Yet we stay
We cling and hold on to the last hanging thread of hope
Maybe it's time we simply let go
Without you, I feel like half of a person
Half of a reason to keep going
A part of me wants to break free from your chains
Chains that have anchored me so low
I thought rock bottom was home
The other part of me, in paradise from our past love
Memories that no scrapbook can ever do justice
Moments I will never get back,
Which half do I choose?

"Alien"

When I drunkenly asked the girl to my side to introduce me to the cutest man in the room,

I would never have thought she would bring me

Face to face

With my other half

Three long years together

Meeting you was the most transformative year of my life

Blossoming from follower to leader

From sheep to lioness

From victim to survivor

My hidden quirks and quench for knowledge revealed itself when I met you,

Like a delicate flower slowly opening up its petals

For the universe to finally witness

You revealed earth's secrets

Hidden truths of the world,

I felt most safe with you.

I always tell people how I never met anybody like you before,

A compliment you've heard so many times now

I question if you're even human.

My love for you is one I do not like to show,

One no soul will ever understand

Cosmic love, beyond this world

Our oddities echo who we are as individuals,

You are my reminder to always stay true to myself.

We've traveled around the world together,

Explored abandoned buildings

Though my favorite abandoned building to explore

Were each other's

We broke down the chains

And explored every corner of one another

From dawn to dusk,

Our past, our future

Our dreams, our goals

Explored until there was nothing left but footsteps

Ours, intertwined

All leading to the front door

The entrance of my home, you are the key

You taught me three important lessons in life

One, how to love my features

Two, to be skeptical of absolutely everything in this world

And three, to always listen to people's stories

Thank you for listening to mine.

When I think of you, my heart doesn't flutter

Instead it dances, like nobody's watching

The freedom of being me, authentically me

Is a side no soul has seen but yours

And when ours souls collide

They don't stop laughing

They don't stop wandering

They don't stop at anything

In fact,

Our problem is that we never seem to know when to stop

But we don't have to be like the rest of them,

We don't have to follow the crowd

We can march to the beat of our drum

As we have, as we will continue to do

There's nobody else quite like us, an unstoppable duo

We may not photograph well together

But we're picture perfect

Always,

In this lifetime

And in the next

"Self"

When you told me your favorite thing about me was

My individuality

I started to like the sound of my name

Each letter, a reminder of who I am

I couldn't recognize the girl in the mirror for so long

And now her reflection couldn't be clearer

I began to love my imperfections

Every flaw, a unique feature only I own,

All mine.

I finally believed I could be somebody

A concept that had felt foreign until I met you

Back then,

No translation would have made sense

I simply didn't understand the language of self love

Now, I'm fluent

Although you're apart from me now,

Your lessons have stayed intact in my well being

In my soul, forever embedded with your words

I love myself,

I can finally say that and mean it

End of Moonlight Confessions,

If you've made it this far, I want to say thank you for reading and purchasing my very first book. I poured my heart & soul into this collection and I genuinely feel like I am finally doing what I was meant to do in this lifetime. I couldn't be happier that you, the reader, not only took the time to read my life story but also read through my poems I have carefully crafted for months now. Thank you for supporting my writing journey and for being you.

Sincerely,

Karin Cho

About The Author

Karin Cho is a Korean-American author, writer, and online blogger from Long Island, New York. She is currently an undergraduate student at the University at Albany majoring in journalism and minoring in psychology. You can find more of her work on medium.com/@karincho.

Instagram: @writerkarin & @karinchox

Made in the USA
Coppell, TX
17 April 2021

54004635R00040